Monday Morning Living

DR. REBECCA R. JACOBSON

CROSSBOOKS
PUBLISHING

CrossBooks™
A Division of LifeWay
1663 Liberty Drive
Bloomington, IN 47403
www.crossbooks.com
Phone: 1-866-879-0502

First published by CrossBooks 9/19/2011

ISBN: 978-1-4627-0614-3 (sc)
ISBN: 978-1-4627-1051-5 (e)
Library of Congress Control Number: 2011915538

Printed in the United States of America
This book is printed on acid-free paper.

Contents

Foreword

Living a life that reflects the values of God's Word is oftentimes difficult at best and seemingly impossible at worst. We are all humans who constantly have to deal with our sinful nature on a personal level. In addition, there is the world we daily live and labor in. The fact is, life's unforeseen circumstances can ruin a perfectly good day—or a perfectly good life: loss of a job, having an accident or health issue, surviving a divorce or death of a family member or friend ... the list is endless.

It is during times like these that questions may arise: Why did God allow this to happen to me? How can I live an "overcoming" life under these circumstances? Can God really forgive me after all I've done? What *is* God's will for my life? What if I missed God's perfect will for my life? Am I doomed to go through this life in God's "permissive" will?

These are just a few of the questions we have all asked at one time or another—whether we have vocalized them or just thought them. Answers to these questions and many more can be found in numerous places. Certainly God's Word is the primary source and can be supplemented with other sources to include books, pastors, counselors, family, and friends, to name a few. The advice and information we get from these sources need to align with God's Word and be of a practical nature so we can apply it to our daily lives—be "livable."

During the sixty-plus years of my life I have read many books searching for practical ways to apply God's Word to my daily life. There are only a handful I've kept to reread because they have been so meaningful and practical on my walk with God. My pastor has often said, "If every day was Sunday, then living for God would be easy." In *Monday Morning Living*, Bec successfully deals with many issues and questions we deal with on a daily basis, providing practical advice on how to live a life that reflects the values of God's Word. *Monday Morning Living* will take its place with the others in that handful of books I will reread time and again.

—Jim Morris, one of God's servants

President and CEO, bitSPATE LLC
Adjunct Professor, University of Tulsa

Preface

During my life, I have had the opportunity to teach in a variety of settings, from Bible studies to the university classroom, from continuing education workshops to women's meetings, and it has been an honor and a privilege. I often learn as much as I offer but have been asked repeatedly if I have written a book so that the things I share could be reviewed on a personal basis. This is my humble attempt at providing a written account of the lessons I have lived—and hopefully have learned something from.

Chapter 1:

Why Does Life Have to Be so Hard?

At some point along the Christian journey, I think most Christians have asked "Why does life have to be so hard? And why does living for God have to be hard?" Some have even given up on their faith walk because it seems impossible to achieve the goal of "true Christian living." Others just get tired of "trying to be perfect." Sunday services are great, even inspirational. It is easy to pacify our minds by attending the services once or twice on Sunday, but then Monday comes along, starting a new week of "busy" that doesn't always reflect the core values we enjoyed the day before.

Or does it? What does "Sunday service" mean to you? Is it a time to "report to God" and get a "check mark," showing that you have attended? Are you there to hear what the preacher has to say and to get your weekly "God information" (like taking a "spiritual vitamin")? Are you there to fulfill your choir duty? Has Sunday service become a tradition that makes you feel better just because you went? None of these reasons are "wrong"; however, these reasons alone do not provide the total amount of strength you will need to face the week ahead. Sunday should be a time of refreshing and gaining strength for the week (or in my case *weak!*). Believers go to church in obedience to God's word. There is nothing wrong with that.

But there can be so much more. Think for a moment about someone in this world who has done something great and costly for you. You thank the person, probably many times, for what he has done. The recipient of an act of kindness will then reflect (and often speak to others) about the character of the person who has done a kind deed or given so much. The one who has given had to be a kind, honest, caring (the list goes on) person in order to help you. Most believers do not have any problem with thanksgiving to God. They understand the cost of their sinful lives and know they could not pay the price for all they have done. But sometimes I wonder how many believers attempt to understand the character of God. Praise is given to God for *what* he has done. Worship is given to God for *who* he is: I Am, that I Am; the creator of heaven and earth and all that is therein (Ps 146:6).

Worship comes from the heart, so there is no "right or wrong" way to worship. However, people often base their worship on how *they feel* instead of who God is. It does not matter how we feel; God does not change and does deserve our worship. The refreshing time comes when we allow our minds to focus on *who* God is and not on who we are, what we have done, how the morning went, or any of the many other complications in life. Trying to be ready to worship makes worship hard; dropping your "issues" and refocusing on who God *is* makes worship easy.

How different is the average life today from those reflected in the Scriptures? Technology has brought convenience, but has it eliminated daily stress? It may have *changed* what people become stressed about, but how much different is "stress" from one generation to another? The new Webster's Dictionary defines stress as "1.) the state of an elastic body under conditions of strain (this must be referring to the young because my body has not been "elastic" for a very long time!), 2.) a state in which a strong demand is made on the nervous system (now they're speaking my language), and 3.) special emphasis given to something (this would be the "stuff" we do every day)." Regardless of the type of stress you live with, it does have an effect on the body, mind, and spirit.

Bodies under stress experience a physical reaction, creating a chemical and physical chain of events. When you are under stress, your body's first reactions are a rise in blood pressure, quicker breathing, increased perspiration, quicker heartbeat, and dilated pupils (Smith and Pergola, 2006). Your senses go on high alert. These physiological changes are part of the body's natural fight-or-flight response. This reaction is instinctive and designed to protect us from threats to our survival. In today's world we are more likely to experience threats to our emotional and mental well-being than our physical safety. Still, the body reacts in the same way: It speeds up to produce energy and get ready to move. The body stays keyed up until the danger passes and then returns to a state of calmness. However, if high levels of stress continue, the body stays agitated, and this can lead to problems. When the body no longer has the energy to adapt to stay at a higher activation from chronic stress, it becomes exhausted. This damages the body's organs in a variety of ways, creating health problems including high blood pressure, heart trouble, asthma, fatigue, and muscle pain as a result of chronic stress. If stress is not relieved, it can cause emotional problems, such as anxiety or depression.

If the physical consequences are not enough to cause concern, the effects on your mind and spirit may begin to cause chronic negative thinking about stress issues and the associated physical problems. Chronic stress causes behavioral, endocrine, immune, and neurotransmitter changes qualitatively similar to those observed in individuals diagnosed with major depression (Leonard, 2001). Anxiety has a number of causes, as well as physical consequences, but the continued rapid pace of daily life and the lack of time for relaxation is often a major contributing factor.

When we encounter a stressful situation, rumination takes over our minds and becomes one of constant focus on how horrible the issue is and how tired the body is, and there will be constant mental juggling of the issue to try and create possible solutions. Rumination and prayer become intermingled, and then condemnation invades the mind, blaming you for not being able to "just let it go" (Arkoff, 1995). This is referred to as "cherished obstacles." Cherished obstacles are situations individuals use to rationalize and excuse their own behavior, because a solution to the problem would require the individuals to face and eliminate what they are contributing to the problem. This is easy to say but not always easy to do. Believers need to develop coping skills to recognize and

4

handle the chain of events that lead to and follow stressful situations, as well as to evaluate and accept responsibility for the stress they may be creating in their own lives. This becomes empowering, because if you are creating the stress, you can control or even eliminate it.

Finally, "spiritual stress" is often the last thing believers focus on because they are not "supposed" to have it. However, years of Christian "rules and regulations" create a form of spiritual stress. Stop and ask yourself: Who made the rule that is running through your mind, creating negative feelings? Where did it come from? Was it really from the Bible? If so, get out your Bible and find it. Read more about it. Understand it in the context in which it was written. Read what happens before it and then continue to read what the Scriptures have to say after the "rule." Think about the culture and "story" surrounding the rule. Scriptures provide guidance, protection, comfort, and a host of positive tools for the believer, but many believers have built their "rules for living" on incomplete passages of Scripture and what someone else tells them the Bible says. When that happens, mental "rules" are created, in turn creating chains of bondage that lead to the idea that, "a daily walk of faith is just too hard!"

The reality is that life is hard, and you can choose to walk through life with the comfort of God's Word or with the stress of trying to make your own comfort. The thought of "the 'stress' of making your own comfort" may seem ironic, but just stop and think for a moment about the many ways people "self-comfort" while experiencing stress. Looking back at childhood or at young children today, a pattern of self-comfort can be seen. Some children suck their thumb, some twirl their hair, some have a blanket or toy they take everywhere, some want to be held, and some sing a little song, just to name a few. As people age, they "trade off" on types of self-comfort. "Treats" and "toys" become rewards for self-comfort for our children, and the blanket gets traded for a special doll or teddy. As children grow older, bonding occurs with a best friend or family member, music is chosen as "my kind of music," and fashion often represents acceptance, which in turn provides the self-comfort that "I am cool." In the adult world, self-comfort continues to take place. Food (now there's a self-comfort issue), shopping, smoking, sex, and pornography can all become a form of self-comfort. Believers may easily (at least outwardly) shun the smoking and sex but will protect the eating and shopping, even when they create health or financial problems. This is what I am referring to when I say "the stress of making your own comfort." The things you do to bring comfort to yourself can create stress in your life.

How do people get off the comfort/stress cycle? There is only one way: self-control. Scripture talks about self-control as being a "fruit" of the spirit. Galatians 5:22-23 states, "But the fruit of the Spirit is love, joy, peace, longsuffering, gentleness, goodness, faith, meekness, temperance: against such there is no law." In order for the spirit to rule over the mind and the body, the spirit must be strong. In order to give strength to the spirit, it must be fed. Scriptures indicate man is divided into three parts (Watchman Nee, 1977).

"And the very God of peace sanctify you wholly; your whole spirit and soul and body be preserved blameless unto the coming of our Lord Jesus Christ"—1 Thessalonians 5:23 NIV.

Where can you find daily nourishment to strengthen your spirit? Read the Word of God.

Chapter 2:

It's Water; Just Drink It!

Many times people say they don't have time to read and study the Bible. First of all, reading the Bible is one thing, and studying it is another. The Word of God is powerful and does mighty things for the believer, but each and every believer must "consume" the Word. Think for a minute about the process of drinking water. When an individual drinks a bottle of water, does that individual "make it work" in their body? Do they analyze every detail and microbe that could be in the water? Do they determine how it will nourish their body? Do they ponder the intentions of the manufacturer? I'm guessing no. They just drink it and trust that it will do what it is supposed to do for their bodies.

The Word of God is the same way. If you just take time to read the Word of God on a daily basis, it is "living water" and will "do" in you what it is supposed to do. God alone has the power to "make it work," but if we do not consume the Word, there is nothing within us for God to work with.

As a child, many believers attended church, memorized Scriptures, sang songs about the Scriptures, and just read Bible stories. They did not think about the "pressure" to understand and interpret everything they read. They did not feel a need to explain or prove to others how much they knew. They just allowed those experiences to become part of their simple lives. We are children of God. It is our job to consume the Word of God; it is *his* job to make it work in us.

Too many Christians are living life on what I would call "spiritual snacks." They attend church (which is important) and listen to media preachers (which can also provide encouragement) and then expect these spiritual "snacks" to sustain and support their belief system. Those same people would never expect to sustain a healthy body by living on snack food. The foundation of every belief system should be based on daily consumption of the Word of God, not "weekly snacks" provided by other godly men and women. If snack food is the basis of your physical diet, you are destined for weight problems and eventually some serious health problems. Those believers who live on spiritual snack food are destined for spiritual problems. Many American believers are living on "spiritual snack food" and do not have the spiritual strength they need to overcome the evil one. They are living in a state of weakness and do not even realize it.

The Bible tells believers that trials and tribulations will come: Many are the afflictions of the righteous: but the Lord delivereth him out of the all.—Psalm 34:19. But I think many believers are having a hard time spiritually due to spiritual weakness and starvation as a result of a lack of daily nourishment from God's Word. Once again, this does not have to be a difficult task of the daily Christian life. Most people eat every single day without making it "hard." Reading God's word, whether it is five verses or two chapters, is not hard when you approach it as consumption. If I consume the Word of God, *He* will make it work.

C. S. Lewis once wrote that we live in the land of the enemy (1984). Take a moment and think about this. Think about any country torn apart by war over religious values. The faction in control does not allow those who disagree to have the freedom to live a life of ease. Those who disagree with the controlling power must be ready for conflict at any time. They must prepare for inconvenience and even suffering. They must know what they believe to the point of possible death. The evil one controls this world. He would prefer that believers' live a life of "spiritual snack food" so they are unprepared and full of empty "spiritual calories" when he attacks their lives. It is time to accept the responsibility that we are the current army of God. Discipline and self-control, as well as personal inconvenience, are accepted as part of the lifestyle when men and women join any branch of military service. Joining God's army is also a choice. As mature believers, we need to accept the responsibility that comes with our choice to serve. God's Word provides us with all that we need to fulfill that requirement.

Galatians 5:22-26 offers direction and lists the fruit that we are given for strength of Christian character: "But the fruit of the Spirit is love, joy, patience, kindness, gentleness and self-control. Against such things there is no law. Those who belong to Christ Jesus have crucified the sinful nature with its passions and desires. Since we live by the Spirit, let us keep in step with the Spirit. Let us not become conceited, provoking and envying each other."

Take a moment and examine these qualities. The first quality listed is love. Who do you love? Those who are exactly like you? Those who believe exactly the way you do? How much love is that? Can you "love" those who are not at all like you? Can you love those who are entangled and trapped by sin, even when they cannot see their way to repentance? Can you worship the God of heaven anywhere at all? Can you worship in any type of church service? Or to you need certain criteria to worship the God you say you love? These are tough questions that I too must ask myself. But joining an "army" is tough. Too often we forget that it is recorded in the Scripture five times that becoming a believer means that we are to "take up a cross" and follow Jesus.

In Matthew 10:34, Jesus says, "Do not suppose that I have come to bring peace to the earth. I did not come to bring peace, but a sword" (believers must carry a weapon— the Word of God—in their hearts and minds).

Jesus goes on to tell of the cost of service in verse 37: Anyone who loves his father or mother more than me is not worthy of me; anyone who loves his son or daughter more than me is not worthy of me: and anyone who does not take his cross and follow me is not worthy of me. Whosoever finds his life will lose it, and whosoever loses his life for my sake will find it—Matthew 10:37-39.

Again in Matthew 16:24-26, Mark 8:34, Luke 9:23, and Luke 14:27: Then Jesus said to his disciples, "If anyone would come after me, he must deny himself and take up his cross and follow me. For whosoever wants to save his life will lose it, but whosoever loses his life for me will find it. What good will it be for a man if he gains the whole world, yet forfeits his soul?"

But wait, you might say, you told us earlier (remember chapter 1?) that it wasn't supposed to be hard to live for God. I would still say it's not hard to live for God. Discipline leads to freedom. Doing whatever "I" want leads to bondage. Let's say I want to live on junk food and never exercise. Is that really freedom? Before too long junk food and a lack of exercise will own me and destroy my body, making it sluggish and out of shape, and then illness will begin to take control. Pick any "vice" and before long that vice will own you. If, however, I choose to control my eating and exercise habits, I am free to engage in a variety of activities. I am even free to have occasional junk food!

Once again it all goes back to the Word of God. If I consume the Word of God daily, it gives me strength for self-control. The Word gives me peace in my spirit even when life is upsetting! Do I live in a floating sense of calm? Of course not, but when crises overtake me, I can run to the author of the Word and find comfort. I can open the pages of Scripture and feed my weary spirit. I can even consume more than my daily dose and gain strength. I can enjoy the refreshing rain of worship just because of *who* He is (yes, I can even worship at home—alone!).

The Word provides comfort that life sometimes is bad simply because we live in the land of the enemy. Pick any of your favorite Bible characters, and you will find a time of overwhelming hardship in their lives. You will find some who wanted to die (David, Elijah), some who lived a long time with pain (Jacob/Israel, Leah, Moses' mother Jochebed), some who did not live to see their prayers answered (Abraham, Joseph, Moses), and many who did not understand how God was working. Where did their strength come from? From the Word of God passed down from generation to generation. It is the Word of God that provides strength and freedom, freedom for living (even during the tough times) in obedience and reaping the blessings of God. Still thinking that maybe the life of the believer is just too hard? Maybe the question you need to ask yourself is, "What exactly am I feeling?"

Chapter 3:

Conviction or Condemnation?

onviction and condemnation are often an ongoing struggle for many believers. First of all, many fail to ask themselves if they are under conviction or condemnation. It is the job of the Holy Spirit to bring conviction to the believer and the unbeliever.

Jesus said in John 16:7-11, "But I tell you the truth: It is for your good that I am going away. Unless I go away, the Counselor will not come to you. When he comes, he will convict the world of guilt in regard to sin and righteousness and judgment: in regard to sin, because men do not believe in me; in regard to righteousness, because I am going to the Father where you can see me no longer; and in regard to judgment, because the prince of this world now stands condemned" (New International Version).

Too often, believers take on the responsibility of "conviction," trying to convince others of what is "right" and what is "wrong." These types of believers think for some reason that they must "be" the Holy Spirit for everyone else. That is where condemnation comes in. Webster's Dictionary defines the root word *condemn* as "to censure, blame, or prescribe punishment for." Since the Word of God is provided as a guide to live by, shouldn't we spend our time understanding the guidelines so we can live by them, rather than interpreting, prescribing, and enforcing them for everyone else?

In counseling, many clients refer to what I call "imaginary rules." For example, I often hear this imaginary rule: "I am not a good parent." I then ask, "What is a 'good parent,' and who made the rules for parenting?" Again, apart from the Word of God, I am not sure you could find an accurate "parenting rulebook." There are some great books that provide "insight," but no child is born with a handbook. When considering "condemnation," too many believers live a lifestyle of bondage based on "imaginary" rules. For example how many times have you heard someone say, "If they were a good Christian they would or wouldn't ___" (you can fill in the blank).

So what exactly is a "good Christian"? Matthew 19 and Mark 10 tell a story of a man who approached Jesus asking about eternal life. Jesus replied to the man (who called Jesus a "good teacher") with, "Why do you call me good?" and then further said, "No one is good except God alone." This idea could be used as an excuse for a variety of sin and imperfect living so before we travel that path let me say this: Believers are called to live a life of obedience to God's word. In order to do that, they need to know God's word. What is the best way to know it? Digest it daily and replace imaginary "rules" with the comfort of God's word so you can live the life of godliness and contentment, which the Bible tells us is "great gain"—1 Timothy 6:6.

Chapter 4:

Behind the Veil

Trying to follow imaginary rules can lead to a life of what I refer to as "prescription" living. Prescription living creates a mask or a veil, which believers then live behind. When you hear the word *veil,* most often it brings about the thought of a wedding dress and wedding ceremony. Most little girls have all dreamed of a wedding day. Think for a minute about what your dreams once were (or maybe still are). One day you would put on a beautiful dress and a beautiful veil and present yourself to the one you love.

Or you might anticipate standing in the church waiting for the one that you so deeply love to come down the aisle. Think about the bride for a moment. Is she excited? Is she waiting with anticipation? Is she prepared physically, emotionally, and intellectually for what she is about to experience? What about the groom? Is he full of anticipation? Or are they just accepting what has been "prescribed" for them? Was this moment in their life chosen years ago, and now they just stand there "going through the motions"?

Once again the Bible provides insight through an example of a story you may know, Jacob and his two weddings. Jacob's first bride was Leah—not exactly what he had expected, but think about her for a moment. What was that wedding day like for her? She was living behind a "prescribed veil" and living in the shadow of a "beautiful" sister. Her marriage to Jacob was a requirement (by her father) and *not* an act of love. She was going through the required and prescribed motions provided by her culture. What were her emotions on that day? Disappointment that she had been forced into the relationship? Fear of rejection by her groom? Anxiety? Depression? Hopelessness? The Bible does not tell us what Leah was feeling the day of or the morning after her wedding. It does, however, tell us that Jacob was *not* happy when he discovered he had married Leah and not Rachel. The Bible does not describe the type of woman Leah was and does not tell us what her thoughts or emotions were, but we can ponder about this. Leah was a bride, but what was behind her veil? Hurt? Pain and a "prescribed life" of rejection? Leah did not make her own choices, yet she fulfilled God's will by becoming the mother of six of the tribes of Israel.

Genesis 29-30 tell about Leah's efforts to "win" the love of her husband and that "Leah was unloved" and the "the Lord has noticed my misery"—Genesis 29:31. What kind of life did Leah have *after* she put on the veil and accepted the prescription? We do not know much, except that she took pleasure in her children and that even though life was directed by the choices of others, she still lived the will of God and fulfilled a very important part of God's plan.

Now consider Jacob for a moment. Leah was not what Jacob expected, and Jacob was angry. Jacob had kept his word and had done everything Laban expected, yet he was still deceived. He too was now in a "commitment" that he had not chosen. Do you think he entered the marriage relationship with words of encouragement for Leah? Do you think he "met her needs" and cherished her? Or did they simply live a life of coexistence? Remember, the Scriptures say that Leah was "unloved" and that Jacob loved her sister, Rachel, so much that seven years of labor "seemed to him but a few days" (Genesis 29:28).

Now stop and reflect on your own life. Where did your veil of prescription come from? Did your parents prescribe what you should be like? Does your "church" prescribe your worship and define your Christian walk? Do imaginary rules define who you are, what you *should* be, and how you *should* live? Have you ever wondered if God has noticed your misery? Prescription living does not always lead to happiness and fulfillment, but that does not mean you cannot be used to fulfill God's plan.

Bride number two for Jacob was Rachel. Jacob loved her dearly and paid a high price for her. What was their wedding day like? One week later, in the shadow of her sister's wedding to the man Rachel loved, she too became Jacob's wife. The Bible says she was beautiful and desired. But what was really behind her veil? Once again we are not given details as to what Rachel felt, but we can glean some insight from the story. She was jealous of her sister and that Leah had children. She was desperate to compete with Leah and blamed her husband for not "giving" her children (Genesis 30:1). She gave her handmaid to her husband so that Rachel could take those children as her own. She "sold" a night with her husband to her sister for "mandrake roots" (Genesis 30:15).Back then mandrakes roots were believed that they could ensure conception. One way or another Rachel got what she wanted. How did she respond to the man who loved her enough to work an extra seven years for her? She traded him for mandrakes. She also had "hidden gods" stolen from her father and then lied to her father and husband to keep them. She too was living behind a veil. Not the same veil as Leah but still a destructive veil. Did her choices prevent God's plan? No, she was also the mother of two of the tribes of Israel, and of Joseph, a story most children know.

There are two more women in this story who are often overlooked: Bilhah and Zilpah. These women are overlooked and forgotten but are important to the Kingdom of God. They gave birth to four of Jacob's children and had to surrender those children to be raised by other women. Today we might compare it to an "open" adoption, where a child will know both the "birth mother" and the woman who had the privilege of raising the child. Do these women matter less because we are not *aware* of what they have done? Clearly that is not the case.

Now think about yourself for a moment. Are you living behind a veil? Maybe it is a veil of expectations and prescription. Maybe it is a veil of deceit. Maybe it is a veil of performance. Maybe it is a veil of religion. Many people live behind a variety of veils for a variety of reasons. What *is* your veil? And what is really behind it? Are you like Leah, feeling trapped in a life of loneliness and prescription? Are you Rachel, looking great on the outside but not finding satisfaction within? Or maybe you are just feeling "overlooked." I believe that God wants us to be the person *he* designed us to be.

Here is Psalm 139. Please take time to *read it* and reflect on each verse.

1) O LORD, you have searched me and known me.

2) You know when I sit down and when I rise up; you understand my thought from afar.

3) You scrutinize my path and my lying down, and are intimately acquainted with all my ways.

4) Even before there is a word on my tongue, behold, O LORD, You know it all.

5) You have enclosed me behind and before, and laid Your hand upon me.

6) Such knowledge is too wonderful for me; it is too high, I cannot attain to it.

7) Where can I go from Your Spirit? Or where can I flee from Your presence?

8) If I ascend to heaven, You are there; if I make my bed in Sheol, behold, You are there.

9) If I take the wings of the dawn, If I dwell in the remotest part of the sea,

10) Even there Your hand will lead me, And Your right hand will lay hold of me.

11) If I say, "Surely the darkness will overwhelm me, And the light around me will be night,"

12) Even the darkness is not dark to You, And the night is as bright as the day darkness and light are alike to You.

13) For You formed my inward parts; You wove me in my mother's womb.

14) I will give thanks to You, for I am fearfully and wonderfully made; wonderful are Your works, and my soul knows it very well.

15) My frame was not hidden from You, When I was made in secret, And skillfully wrought in the depths of the earth;

16) Your eyes have seen my unformed substance; and in Your book were all written the days that were ordained for me, when as yet there was not one of them.

17) How precious also are Your thoughts to me, O God! How vast is the sum of them!

18) If I should count them, they would outnumber the sand when I awake, I am still with You.

19) O that You would slay the wicked, O God; Depart from me, therefore, men of bloodshed.

20) For they speak against You wickedly, and Your enemies take Your name in vain.

21) Do I not hate those who hate You, O LORD? And do I not loathe those who rise up against You?

22) I hate them with the utmost hatred; they have become my enemies.

23) Search me, O God, and know my heart; try me and know my anxious thoughts;

24) And see if there be any hurtful way in me, and lead me in the everlasting way.

(Source: BibleGateway.com)

This says *God* made *you* in your mother's womb. Did he make a mistake? Did he "slip" when it came to your unique personality? Psalm 139:16 tells us he knew us before we were born: "Your eyes saw my unformed body; all the days ordained for me were written in your book before one of them came to be." We have heard so often that "God is the God of second chances" and that somehow, if we miss "plan A" we have changed "God's plan." Or maybe you think that God will put together a "plan B" for your life. I prefer to say that God is God and that he knows how to bring about his will in the life of his people, despite our poor choices. Enoch and Elijah are the only people other than Jesus who did not make poor choices. Our choices bring consequences to our lives that we may have to endure until eternity, but God makes crooked paths straight and is powerful enough to fulfill His plan if our hearts and lives have been given to him. Even poor choices can be used to remind of us of our need for Jesus as Lord and Savior. Poor choices help us "live" the concepts of "mercy" and "grace."

Ruth and Ester are women many Christians are familiar with. We know the stories of hard choices that God used to fulfill his plan. And yes, there are believers who make "hard" choices and fulfill God's plan. But we need to understand that Leah, Bilhah, and Zilpah had others make choices for their lives, and God fulfilled his plan. Even Rachel was used

23

by God to fulfill his plan. Can I explain how? Not really. That is why God is God and God is so much bigger than my understanding.

⋎ What types of choices have you made? Give them to God and allow him to fulfill his plan; trust that he will make your crooked paths straight and that his power is greater than your choices. Commit to making the best choices you can and then believe that God will not be limited in his ability.

Jesus tells us we must become "like little children" to inherit the kingdom of God. Matthew 18:3-4 states, "Verily I say unto you, except ye be converted, and become as little children, ye shall not enter the kingdom of heaven. Whosoever, therefore shall humble himself as this little child, the same is the greatest in kingdom of heaven." Think about young children. Do they evaluate every choice they make? Are they perfect? Do they worry about what others will think? Do they like themselves? Do they point out others' imperfections? Are they "afraid" when they are with their father or mother? Do they honestly show you who they are? Do they expect failure? That same passage goes on to "warn" about offending childlike believers as well. Little children are not living behind any veils. They are not living a life of prescription. They do not expect their choices to limit their parents' ability to keep life running smoothly. They are free in the confidence that their loving parents will protect them and will fix anything and everything.

⋏ Often when you watch children play it can be seen that children *love* to obey when they clearly know it will make their Mom and Dad happy. Ephesians 5:1 tells us to "Be ye therefore followers of God, as dear children, and walk in love as Christ also hath loved us, and hath given himself for us an offering and a sacrifice to God for a sweet smelling savor." Young children *love* to serve. Have you ever been to a tea party with a five-year-old? All she wants is your time and approval. Children do not focus on what they believe they have done wrong; they just try and fix it. And if they can't fix it, they believe their Mom or Dad will fix it. Take a moment and think about yourself at five or six years old. What were you like? Did you "like" who you were? Ask any kindergarten child if he or she can draw, dance, or sing. What will the answer be? Yes to any of those questions! Children do not measure *who* they are by performance. They have to be taught that the quality of their performance matters. As a matter of fact, if you ask them who they are, the first answer they will give is their *name.*

I have asked countless adults and students, "Who are you?" and get a list of performance answers, including mother, father, student, wife, daughter, nurse, and accountant—the list is endless. I then ask them to remove *all* performance descriptions from their list, and all too often there is nothing left. Many did not even put their *name* on the list. Their busy lives and the prescription of performance have pushed out who they are. Life has exchanged the "who we are" for "what we do." And when what we do is gone, what is left? Who did God design you to be?

I am not asking, "What did God design you to do?" That question is meaningless if you are not "becoming" who God designed you to be. Are you being the "person" God designed you to be? Or are you hiding behind a veil of prescription that the world has given you? Maybe you are hiding behind a "believer" or religious veil. God knows who he designed you to be, and he did *not* mess up your personality when he designed you. He knows all about the veil you are wearing and what you are trying to hide. Guess what? He loves you more than Jacob loved Rachel. He is waiting with excitement and expectation for the day you will be together.

But are you prepared? Are you becoming the person he formed in your mother's womb? *When you stand before Jesus preparing for that wedding day,* who *is behind the veil?* Is it the "person" God knows, is longing for, and expects? Or is it an anxious, uncertain person who is trying to fulfill the veil of performance and prescription? As we become the person God has designed us to be, we move toward living the will of God.

Chapter 5:

God's Will ... Can You Find It?

I have heard many God-loving preachers talk about "finding the will of God" for your life. And for many years as a young person, I struggled and prayed and cried over that very issue. I would ask, "How do you find the will of God?" The answer: Pray, and God will lead you. I now believe I was given that answer because there was a lack of understanding about the will of God by myself and those kind people who were trying to answer. And that answer is not necessarily "wrong."

Once again, however, the answer is found in the Word of God. Let's take a look at some women in the Bible and see whether they "found" the will of God. The book of Ruth tells the story of this wonderful woman who made some hard choices. Ruth made a choice that was not "prescribed" for her. It was not "common" for women who had lost their husbands to stay with their mothers-in-law. The prescribed thing for the widow to do was return to her family. Ruth *chose* to stay with her mother-in-law and accept that family as her own. Once again we are not provided the details about what Ruth was thinking or feeling. But we do know this: Her place in history came from a decision that was not prescribed. Ruth followed the desires of her heart and allowed God's will to unfold. Do you think her journey began with the "hopes" of finding God's will? Or was she following her heart?

Many have heard the story of Ester, of her beauty and bravery. Ester made choices that were not prescribed. She allowed procedure to guide the way she carried out her choices, but she did not conform to the prescribed social procedures of self-protection. She made a *choice* to ask the king for mercy for her people. It was not the common thing for women to do, and Ester could have died as a result of her choice. Ester took her place in history as well by "being Ester" and allowing God's will for her life to unfold.

Rahab was another woman who had a place in Biblical history. Rahab was not even what could be considered a "chosen one of God." And yet she too ended up "in the will of God" by making choices that clearly were not prescribed by those around her. She provided a hiding place for two spies, not knowing that this was her "place" in God's will. A moment, one line in a story, was the "Will of God" for Rahab.

We work so hard at "finding God's will" when what we need to do is "be" the person God designed us to be and allow God's will to unfold on a daily basis. That begins with recognition of our need for God as a sinner. I don't know that any of these women were trying to "find" or "do" the will of God. These women were "being," and in being who God designed them to be, they "did" what God designed for them. In their lifetime, were they "aware" they had "found" the Will of God? I doubt it. Did they "feel" God's direction? I don't know, but the Bible doesn't tell us.

There is nothing "wrong" with feelings—I happen to have many of them! But feelings are a result of living, not *direction* for living. Feelings are an experience and are not "right" or "wrong." They simply accompany the moment. I constantly encourage students to feel "free" to experience their own emotions, because emotions are not "bad"— behavior is.

Scripture tells us, "Be angry [emotion] and sin not [behavior follows the statement]: let not the sun go down upon your wrath: Neither give place to the devil"—Ephesians 4:26-27. Our actions, not emotions, become sin. I encourage students and clients to experience their emotions. Emotions are part of who you are. The important step is to learn to *control* your actions until your emotions have passed (now that's the hard part). We have one important "choice" in life, and that is to surrender our hearts to God and accept Jesus as Savior and Lord of our hearts. Then we are "free" to experience life knowing that we are covered by the blood, mercy, and grace of Jesus. When Jesus was teaching the disciples to pray, he did not tell them pray to "find God's will."

"The Lord's Prayer," which is so familiar to many believers, follows. This is how you should pray:

"Our Father who art in heaven, hallowed be your name. Thy kingdom come, thy will be done on earth as it is in heaven. Give us today our daily bread. Forgive us our debts as we also have forgiven our debtors. And lead us not into temptation but deliver us from the evil one, for yours is the kingdom, and the power, and the glory now and forever. Amen"—Matthew 6:9-13.

As you reflect on the words of Jesus, you will not find the admonition to ask God to "show" you his will. The prayer states, "Thy will be done." Jesus himself, in his own time of desperation, prayed, "Not my will but thine."

Chapter 6:

Why Did this Happen To Me?

Even in the process of living God's will we encounter negative and often unexplainable events. When this occurs, there are "pat" Christian answers that are given by well-meaning friends, such as "It was God's will" or "Just pray about it and Jesus will take care of it." Now those sayings may be true but often do not bring much comfort, because deep inside some voice is telling us that there "must" be a reason this is happening. Too often our minds will ruminate until we invent a "reason" that will satisfy and accommodate our belief system. However, when I work with people who have just lived through the unexplainable, I often tell them that "trash" is part of life. Think for a moment about your home. Everyday living creates "trash" in your home. Good people, bad people, godly people, and ungodly people all have trash. It is a function of living. Sometimes tragic events happen, and the only reason is that we are "living in the land of the enemy" and life has provided some "unexpected trash."

The Bible tells us that Satan has come to "kill, steal, and destroy" (John 10:10). That is his job, regardless of what type of person you are, or what your "belief" system is. He has done this throughout time and is very good at it. No one is exempt, and salvation does not prevent tragedies in life. Our relationship with God, through salvation and knowledge of his word, provides a "coping card," not an "exemption card." Too many people are filled with guilt and self-torment because they think an unexpected crisis would not happen if they just believed in God a little more. But that is not the case. Faith is not an exemption card from life crisis; it is what I call a "coping card to deal with crisis" No one is exempt from tragedy.

As I was finishing my PhD, working on my dissertation and facing written and oral comprehensive exams, my family lived through four tragedies that occurred within one year. The first, my sister-in law died in an automobile accident, leaving behind a husband and five children. Six months later, two of my twenty-year-old nieces were in an automobile accident on their way home from a church event. One went to be with the Lord, and the other faced years of physical recovery and possible permanent disability. Three months later my father died of heart failure, and my mom's sister was diagnosed with colon caner and died shortly thereafter.

At the time, my oldest son was eight years old and was very close to two of the people who died. My niece was twenty years old and like a sister to him. She would pick him up from school and take him to Taco Bell. My dad was his only living grandfather and was his special "Hooty Tooty Grampa." After their deaths (which were within six months of each other), I would take him to school, and every day he would cry and beg me to just wait in the parking lot until he was done for the day. He didn't want me to be in an accident and die. He attended a Christian school, and many well-meaning people would tell him that I would be okay and Jesus would keep me safe. But in his world, *Jesus* was the one who took a mother from her children, his cousin (who picked him up from school every day), and his Grampa. Those well-meaning people would make up reasons and tell him that it had been time for his family to leave and be with Jesus. This was a very painful time for me as well, trying to help my son understand what we had just lived through.

Our family's grief was overwhelming, yet others wanted us to just "move us along." I look back and ask myself, Why? Why as a culture do we try and "speed up" and explain tragedy? Why do we always need a "reason" for everything bad? We (my husband, children, and I) learned through some very tough life experiences that sometimes there is *no* reason and that God is bigger than our minds. God allowed four people in our family to move to eternity within one year. We may not understand *the reasons,* but our commission as believers is not to "understand God" but to obey God. And truthfully, we, like so many believers, don't like obedience unless it "feels" good. Obedience does not always "feel" right or good. Check with Abraham and many of the other saints in the Bible. How did it "feel" to take your only son, the promise of God, up a mountain to be sacrificed? How did it feel to place your baby in a basket in a dangerous river?

Now, as a psychologist and counselor, I do have to help clients deal with negative experiences and the "feelings" that accompany those experiences. Some negative experiences (like those just mentioned) are out of our control. Others can be a result of poor life choices. As a counselor and parent, I advocate personal responsibility and choices that are wise based on the information you have at the time of the choice. And if actions bring negative consequences, then learn to accept and handle the consequences that your choices brought. However, most of the time, we do not get to "choose" the negative events that are a part of living. I refer to this in counseling as "trash."

Life's trash can be an "unexpected" consequence of our own choice, it can be the result of a loved one's poor choices, or it can simply be a lapse in judgment and the inability to foresee the consequences. Regardless, we must learn to deal with "life's trash" and understand the grace and mercy of God. I tell my boys that "mercy" is when you deserve negative consequences but have escaped them and that "grace" is given to you by God to carry you through the consequences of poor choices. God is abundant with both. "My grace is sufficient for thee"—2 Corinthians 12:9. Trying to determine a "reason" for all the "trash in life" is a game that can lead to a quagmire of unnecessary guilt and rumination about "should-haves." Learning to accept that life makes "trash" and that everyone must learn (learning is what occurs when what we thought would work didn't) to handle it appropriately can provide a sense of assurance that God has not forgotten us during the tough times. Once again it is in knowing the Word of God that you will find strength, comfort, and instruction that will carry you through hard times.

James 5:16 states: "Confess your faults one to another, and pray one for another, that ye may be healed. The effectual fervent prayer of a righteous man availeth much." These "unexplainable" and difficult times in life often create in those who live through them the ability to "fervently" pray for others without trying to "reason" why the event is happening. In other words, you can "recycle" your "trash" into the ability to pray "effectual prayers" for others.

Chapter 7:

Go Figure????

Unexplainable negative life events are often the times that send us back to the Word of God. Daily reading of God's Word will enhance your life and mind in many ways and provide a "new look" at some of the same old stories. Often, as we reread stories that we have heard so many times, questions develop. Sometimes these questions are "unanswerable" but even then can serve a positive purpose in your walk with God. Looking at Bible dilemmas can provide peace in the confusing circumstances of our own lives. These are the times that I refer to as "go figure" times, because they just don't make sense. I will share a few of my favorite Bible "go figure" stories that you may be able to relate to.

The story of Joseph is one familiar to many believers. He had many "go figure" moments throughout his life. Here is a young man who had his birth mother die when he was a boy. Imagine that. Then there were severe family problems (as large families often have) between him and his siblings that resulted in a "pitfall" in his life. The story continues, and Joseph moves into Potiphar's house, makes the "right choices," but still ends up living in a dungeon for years (not just a few days). I can't help but think if this was a modern-day story of a believer's life experience, well-meaning "friends" would be generating all types of "reasons" for each event. When in reality, the reason Joseph went to that dungeon still remains unclear, with the exception that it was "God's plan," and God didn't choose to explain why. Again, I know all the details of the story, but Joseph didn't have the entire detailed plan. Surely God could have taken him from living in Potiphar's house to interpret those dreams or even have given Joseph his own dream so that he would have assurance that he was "in the Will of God."

But that is not how the story goes. Joseph had to live each day and trust the God he believed in would not forsake him. Joseph got out of that dungeon and then lived like an Egyptian without abandonment of his personal faith, eventually making a way for God's chosen people. As we read these stories, we need to stop and reflect on the "moment" of the story. How did Joseph respond in each negative or even positive "moment" throughout this story? In each circumstance or moment of time, Joseph believed God's word. As believers, that is all we are given—a moment in time. As we live each of those moments, being the person God has designed us to be, living through the events he has allowed, trusting his word, our lives becomes a piece of his divine "story."

The story of Moses also begins with a "go figure" event. Moses was placed in the Nile River as his sister watched from the shore. God allowed (or directed) this mother to put her young child in a basket on a dangerous river. How does that make sense? Yes we know that Pharaoh's daughter was bathing and rescued the child, which leads to the next "go figure" point. His mother was his nurse; however, Moses was raised in Pharaoh's house and trained in the ways of the Egyptians. Surely a man who was destined to lead the people of God out of Egypt should have experienced the burden of the people. As the story continues, Moses kills a man, which in turn leads to self-imposed exile from Egypt into a foreign land. He marries and eventually returns to Egypt, and his brother (who was raised as a slave) helped with the actual leadership as the people began their journey to freedom. However, when Moses was placed on the river, no one knew the "rest of the story," and God did not "explain" the entire story to those who were living through it.

Another story that leads to that "go figure" moment is Rahab. The book of Joshua, chapter 2 tells about this prostitute who chose to help the spies Joshua had sent into Jericho. Rahab had a "moment in time" and an encounter with the Spirit of God that changed her life. But her "moment" came while she was a prostitute who was willing to hide two spies and then lie to the government about it. There are many examples in the Bible of "go figure" moments, and I am not going to attempt to explain them. They serve the purpose of showing us that God is working way beyond our understanding and that a walk of faith is just that—walking and trusting God when there is no explanation.

Paul is another example of a man "raised" by the "worldly" or cultural views of his day and then chosen to be a man of God. My point is not to discount those who have been raised in the faith (like Samuel, David, and so many others) but to encourage those who think that because they were not "raised in the church," their service to God is somehow "less valuable" than those who have a legacy of faith that goes back ten generations.

My final "go figure" thought is the story of Jesus and the man at the pool of Bethesda (John 5:1-15). Jesus healed just one man at the pool. He clearly had the power to heal all the people, but we are only told of the one man who had been dealing with illness for thirty-eight years. All the people at the pool had a need, yet we are only told of the one man. Well-meaning people often say, "The man was the only one with faith," but the Bible does not say that. It just says Jesus knew he had been there a long time and turned and asked him, "Wilt thou be made whole?"—John 5:6.

Now Jesus had the power to heal all those people, so why didn't he? For that matter, why didn't he change the life of every single person he encountered? Surely *he* had the power to do that. And yet modern-day believers carry an imaginary weight that we must constantly "provide a life-changing touch" to every person we encounter. Why Jesus did not heal everyone is just another "go figure" moment. I really don't know, and once again the Bible does not provide an explanation. These examples from both the Old and the New Testaments remind me that God is sovereign and is so much greater than my simple level of understanding. That is why we can trust him and surrender our inflexible life plans to simply living for God in this moment according to his Word.

Chapter 8:

Converted Egocentricity

Websters dictionary defines egocentrism as "limited in outlook or concern to one's own activities or needs." In psychology, "egocentrism" is the characteristic of regarding oneself and one's own opinions or interests as most important. The term derives from the Greek egô, meaning "I." An egocentric person cannot "put himself in other people's shoes," and believes everyone sees what he sees (or that what he sees in some way exceeds what others see.) Jean Piaget (1896-1980) claimed that young children are egocentric. This does not mean they are selfish but that they do not have the mental ability to understand that other people may have different opinions and beliefs than they do.

"Converted egocentricity" is what I will define as developing a walk with God that is centered around "myself" rather than "God" and his Word. Now first of all, let me say that there is nothing wrong with seeking God with all of your ability and having a desire to be "full of God."

However, why do you want to be "full" of God? Is your desire to be so "spiritual" that everyone else can see just how spiritual you are? Do you want people to "look" at you so they can then see how much "Jesus is in me"? Are your prayers all about *you* and *your* needs? Do you approach every service with an attitude of "receiving" from God? There are times when we all need is to receive a genuine touch from God. However, what would the purpose of your receiving be? Is it just to make *your* life better? I have tried to teach my children that the primary purpose of service on Sunday is to set time aside to *give* to God. It is a way to show our love by setting aside our busy lives to meet with him. It is in meeting with God that we draw our strength for daily living.

For several years now I have met with a friend once a week for breakfast. We sit for at least two hours and just share time together. We meet, pray, eat, and visit. Most of the time it is an exchange of ideas and information, talking about what has been happening and how we are dealing with life. However, over the years there have been times where individually we have faced trials and the storms of life. During those times, breakfast will focus on the one with the "need." The need is the focus of our conversation, and possible solutions as well as comfort will be shared. This builds the relationship and communicates our love and concern for each other. I don't leave every breakfast meeting asking myself, "What did I get out of that meeting today?" If nothing particularly stressful is happening (just the daily grind) I don't think, *I guess I'll quit going because I am not getting* my *needs met.* The fact is, needs are being met, without evaluation or "cognitive awareness." Whether I "feel" the breakfast food meeting a physical need or not, the process is working. If I "feel" the bond of friendship or not on any given day does not determine the status of the relationship. It is there.

And yet many believers are constantly "evaluating" spirituality based on a Sunday service and how that particular service related to "me" and "my feelings." Believers should gather on Sunday to work as a team. Maybe the service is not about "you" this week. Maybe the service is about someone who has experienced such a terrible loss that they cannot even imagine a loving God, and your purpose in that service is to pray for that emotionally distraught soul you don't even know. Maybe God wants you to come to service to pray for those individuals, whose lives may be in genuine crisis and who are so distraught that they cannot even think to pray. When believers gather together it is a time for the body of Christ to function cohesively. Whenever and wherever my physical body is hurt, the rest of my physical body is designed to work together for the healing of the one area in need. Wouldn't it be wonderful if the body of Christ could gather together and focus on the needs rather than, "What I can get out of the service?"

If believers choose to walk according to God's word, they will be living his Will on a daily basis, and if they will shift from egocentric thinking to genuine concern for the souls of others, their life will be a daily exchange (and not just on Sundays) of God's power through them touching the lives of others. Will they "know it" (have cognitive awareness of it)? At times maybe yes, and at other times no. I have been teaching on many occasions (textbook material that I am commenting on or reflecting about life on), and after class, a student will come up to me and say, "Can I come by your office and talk to you? What you said in class tonight has really made me think about my own life [or belief system], and I have some questions." My mind will immediately begin to race trying to figure out what "I" said. But I have grown to realize that God was working "through" me and was not going to "tell" me what he had used to speak to that person. At that moment, I was "dead" in Christ, and he was speaking to the heart of that student. I did not need to feel or even know what he was doing. I simply needed to "be" an empty vessel whose name was "Dr. J." He was taking an opportunity to further share *his* love with that person in an "unconventional" way. When we strive to be the person God created us to be, then *he* can fulfill his Will through us on a daily basis, and *he* is not "obligated" to provide some kind of "feeling" or foreknowledge about what his Will for that day is going to be.

Chapter 9:

⟨∽⟩

Ghosts and Graveyards

"Being" and not just "doing" may sound strange or even impossible. And often, people who are genuinely trying to live this kind of life find that their past tends to keep creeping into the present and creating obstacles to personal growth. Those past experiences create what I call "ghosts and graveyards." Webster's provides one definition of "ghost" that is appropriate for this discussion: "A mental representation of some haunting experience." Many choices in life create consequences that are not easy to live with. And even when there are not long-term physical consequences, too often there are long-term emotional consequences. Choices that were made many years ago quickly come to mind every time life gets difficult and create a "ghost" that will continue to perplex the mind or call us back to a time in our past.

When counseling individuals, those ghosts and graveyards soon become apparent in a variety of ways. The first most common way is when the client is dealing with a current issue or tragedy. When I ask, "Why do you think that this has happened to you?" the answer often is, "When I was younger I didn't treat my family/friend/etc. right" (pick one—or more). Or, "Years ago, when I was young, I had an abortion," or "I had an affair," or "I committed (some sin)." It is like an historic event (or person) is waiting to punish them for previous life choices that they have repented of and maybe even have already suffered consequences for. Again, I realize that poor physical choices can create physical consequences, but what I am referring to are the lingering thoughts about the past event that continues to shape present choices.

These types of negative historic events need to be placed in the "graveyard" after repentance. What do I mean by *graveyard*? A graveyard is what I refer to as a place that we can "leave" the negative past experiences. Yes, we may have to visit it from time to time (life consequences), but that does not mean we have to live there. An abortion, affair, or divorce are all tragedies that have consequences. But the emotional pain of those events does not have to continually create negative experiences in our present life. God is a God of forgiveness, as well as of creativity.

Therefore if any man be in Christ, he is a new creature: old things are passed away; behold all things are become new—2 Corinthians 5:17. Those experiences can be used to create wisdom and effectual prayer for the present.

One aspect of dealing with graveyards includes "becoming new" and learning to incorporate the fruit of the spirit into our everyday lives. This means taking what we learn on Sunday into Monday and beyond. In bible college, we used to have fun with the Scripture in Romans

12:19, which says in part, "Vengeance is mine; I will repay, saith the Lord," by saying, "Vengeance is mine, I can repay; the Lord says so." Now we were all joking of course, but doesn't that really reflect a version of converted egocentric "self-control"?

"I'll handle it" is another common response to life's pressures. But self-control is genuinely reflected by the entire Scripture in Romans 19, which says in full, Dearly beloved, avenge not yourselves, but rather give place unto wrath; for it is written, vengeance is mine; I will repay, saith the Lord.

So we exercise self-control by controlling our anger in a healthy way and then depending on our God for a solution. Easier said than done, but this should still be a goal for the growing believer.

One of my favorite Bible examples that deals with problems I think every believer will face (if you live long enough and are around other people) can be found in Numbers 12. The chapter begins with, "And Miriam and Aaron spake against Moses because of the Ethiopian woman whom he had married."

Family (we all have them)—they didn't like his spouse ... now there's a modern-day problem. It goes on to show just how spiritual these siblings thought they were in the very next verse. Numbers 12:2 continues with, "And they said, 'Hath the Lord indeed spoken only by Moses? Hath he not also spoken also by us?'"

So even back then family issues encountered a "spiritual twist." In all honesty, most people would jump right into this family argument, defend their position, and waste much time and feelings on *who* is "spiritual" and who is not. But that is not how Moses chose to handle things. Verse 3 tells us that Moses was "meek" and allowed the Lord to handle the situation. If you know the story, you realize that God took some drastic measures, causing Miriam to immediately become leprous and Aaron to beg Moses for forgiveness. Moses did intercede for his siblings, but they still had to suffer consequences for their actions (Numbers 12:9-15). When pondering this example, how many believers today would: a) jump into the family feud; b) claim to be the "most spiritual"; and c) rejoice that "God took my side" and the others had to pay? Oh that people today could learn to be like Moses, especially when it comes to handling family problems. Moses was transparent, allowed God to direct the solution, and did not respond to this problem with a list of his previous performance.

Maybe your life circumstance is so much more than a family member or former friend speaking badly about you. Maybe you have been betrayed by your spouse, a clergy member, or someone else you shared your heart with. In no way would I ever make light of that experience, but take a moment to think about this. Can the offender ever do anything to make it right? Is there really anything he or she can do that will make you let go of the offense? Can another person rebuild trust in you once it is gone? The reality of severe hurt is that you own the pain and it can only be shared with God. Life does not give us a chance to "undo" hurt. We must travel through it, and with the grace of God allow the healing process to take place. Often I hear people say, "Just get over it!" Again, there is no "getting over it," but you can learn to live with it and even allow God to use that experience for inner growth. Does it "feel" good? No, initially, it does not. Have you changed? Yes you have.

However, whether the change is positive or negative is up to you. You hold the power to incorporate, grow, and move on or ruminate, feed the anger, and stagnate. I have lived through betrayal, rejection, and even deceit by loved ones. The details do not matter since the process of healing is the same for all types of emotional loss.

While initially this may sound hard, there is genuine freedom that can be found in the process. Again, the Word of God provides direction. It says in Galatians 2:20, "I have been crucified with Christ and I no longer live, but Christ lives in me. The life I now live in the body, I live by faith in the Son of God, who loved me and gave himself for me."

So I had to ask myself, Can a dead man really be offended? The answer seems obvious enough: no. Well, if I was "dead," why was I in so much emotional pain? That answer was also obvious: I wasn't really "dead" in Christ. I wanted to hang on to the piece of "me" that had been offended. As I worked through that (and yes, it took quite some time, prayer, and Scripture to sort it all out), I realized that since God is the only being who has paid the price of sin and can forgive sin that I could not "hang on to," the sins of others that offended me. Reality is this: I cannot forgive sin because I did not pay the price of sin. And if I am dead in Christ, then no one has sinned against me—the sin and offense is against God. Does this mean I think that those who have caused the hurt need to come right back into your life? *No*, I am not saying that either. There are situations that lead to an end to relationships. And restoration is just not an option. People move forward an begin the healing process with those who can understand and share the pain. Bearing each others' burdens during the healing process.

Chapter 10:

Does Forgiveness Require Reconciliation?

In a relationship with God, forgiveness equals reconciliation. However, people are not just "little gods" who have the power to forgive sin and repair the past. To say we have that ability would say that we are equal with God, which we clearly are not. Also, I have heard it said that "if you are a Christian, you have to forgive me." True, as a believer I need to come to terms with what I have experienced and "let go" of requiring a "payment" for wrongs done. However forgiveness comes with many misconceptions, some of which can be very damaging to individuals who are in unhealthy or hurtful relationships (Wade, 2010). For example, many people think that forgiveness necessarily includes reconciling with the offending person. But just because the Bible tells us to forgive does not mean we must "restore" dangerous or destructive relationships; there are biblical examples where God allowed family separation as part of his plan. God told Abraham to take his wife and children and journey to the land of promise and leave the rest of his family behind. Abraham took with him a nephew named Lot. Over time, Lot's people and Abraham's people could not get along, and so begins the story of Lot's fall, ending with the well-known story of Sodom and Gomorrah. Abraham kept a "family relationship" despite God's direction to leave his family behind.

Ruth is another biblical example of "leaving" family behind and moving forward with an individual life journey. Her husband died, and the custom of that day was for the widow to return to live with her family. However, she chose to defy expectations and travel with her mother-in-law, saying, "Your God will be my God and your people my people." If you are unfamiliar with the story, she eventually becomes the wife of Boaz and is in the lineage of Jesus. There are many other stories, and while forgiveness is necessary in all situations, the point that needs to be made is that not all relationships need to move forward after a crisis. Some do and some don't.

Should you decide that in your situation you need to reconcile, here are some things to think about: Reconciliation in any type of relationship requires a few things, starting with an acknowledgement of the wrong that was done by the offender. Many people attempt reconciliation by beginning with the statement, "If I have done anything wrong ..."

I tell clients there are problems with this type of approach. First of all, *if* can indicate a few things;

1) I have wronged someone and do not have a clue what I did. In which case it is very possible that I will do the same thing to you again and want

you to accept a relationship that includes that possibility.

2) I have wronged someone and know it. But I do not want to accept the responsibility of the wrong or address the painful consequences that followed. And those who have been wronged need to just "get over it" because what happened to you is not important enough to me to re-experience that pain in order to bring healing.

Even salvation requires that we "confess our sins," which is acknowledgement of the wrong we have done. The other comment that I often hear from the offender is, "Let the past be the past." This is an ideal statement, and it would be nice it if it was truly possible with anyone other than God himself. People fail to realize that the past has permanently and irreparably changed the present in positive and negative ways. Healing in relationships requires that both parties face the painful consequences that were a result of the situation. Until both parties face that painful fact, I would not even recommend reconciliation for the relationship because healing has not occurred, and like a wound that has never been treated for infection, the pain is just below the surface and will explode in some other fashion, hurting even more people.

Unless the people involved in the betrayal are willing to work through these initial steps, I see no reason to add to the pain someone is living with. If no one is willing to acknowledge what they have done, then it really is possible that the whole situation could happen all over again, causing more hurt, pain, and discouragement. And generally speaking, the person who has been offended has enough pain in his or her life that he or she is trying to resolve without adding to the uncertainty of facing the hurt again. These individuals are in the process of learning to deal with their current emotions and allowing God to create "new things" in their lives. Is this really possible? Yes! In my life's journey, have I been hurt? Yes, deeply. Do I have scars? You bet, but with time and God's grace those scars are fading. Am I bitter? No, every life must live through some trials, and as we recover, God brings healing and replacement. God will use whatever pain you have survived to bring healing to the lives of others. Is reconciliation with those who created the scars required? Not always, and not until all are willing to follow a genuine process of healing. Even God requires that people admit their sin and turn in a new direction before forgiveness is complete.

Chapter 11:

Flexible Personality

Throughout this life's journey working with people who are dealing with forgiveness, consequences, or life's trials, I have encountered many people who say, "That's just the way I am!" This statement reflects that one's personality is somehow rigid and inflexible. In my office I have some modeling clay that I use for a variety of exercises with the children with whom I work. Take a minute and consider the characteristics of modeling clay: it is flexible and stable at the same time. However, if not cared for the modeling clay can become dried out, hard, or crumbling. Modeling clay cannot "fix itself," but in caring hands moisture can be added and gently worked so that it becomes flexible and usable once again.

Betrayal, hypocrisy, condemnation, "go figure" moments, ghosts and graveyards, and un-forgiveness can all cause us to "dry out" and become hard or crumbling. It takes the hands of caring individuals in our lives to gently add the "moisture" of kind words, faith, and encouragement to once again soften those who have become hardened by life.

Once again the Bible tells us in Galatians 6:1-2: "Brethren, if a man be overtaken in a fault, ye which are spiritual, restore such an one in the spirit of meekness; considering thyself, lest thou also be tempted. Bear ye one another's burdens and so fulfill the Law of Christ."

"A friend loveth at all times, and a brother is born for adversity"—Proverb 17:17 (KJV). This is not an easy task. Loving a "hardened" person means we must be willing to encounter rejection, unfair comments, and sometimes just toxic words without responding negatively to those actions.

Modeling clay is not repaired by "pouring moisture" on it. It must be held and gently worked until it begins to soften. Often this has to be done more than once before it begins to respond and regain usefulness. As a counselor and psychologist, what I often do is provide a "safe place" and just listen, without condoning or condemning. Just being caring hands, adding kindness to hurting people, and allowing God's love and timing to work through the pain that has "dried" out their Spirit. As believers we are to "bear one another's burdens," not discuss, criticize, and instruct each other about the burden. Now I am not saying that sharing personal experience or encouragement are wrong, they're just not always necessary.

Ask yourself this, Do I listen for understanding? Or am I preparing an answer while listening? Am I willing to "carry that burden," or am I wanting to give instruction on how *they* should carry that burden? Too often we are so busy thinking about what "we" are going to say that we miss the heart cry of the person in pain. A client may come in angry and spew all kinds of toxic words, but when I really listen, I hear hurt. I generally respond with, "Wow, that must have really hurt you when that happened" or "I can't imagine how hard that was for you handle all of that pain," and those angry words quickly soften into moist eyes or a flow of tears. Learning to listen to a "heart cry" rather than the words is what the Holy Spirit can teach us if we will take the time to be still and listen to him. Only the Spirit of God and the Word of God can teach us the difference between "reflection of their spirit," "reaction to their words," and "direction of their actions."

Chapter 12:

Life is a River; Hang on and Ride!

Generally speaking, most clients come to the office of a counselor looking for specific direction and a "quick fix" to a lifelong problem. Since I am not the "answer man," I have to help them understand that their life experience is unique and that like a river, they have to learn how to deal with it and ride it out. Even I had to learn this, and it was one of the most important lessons I learned. And yes, even my life is sometimes like riding a river. (Even counselors and psychologists have to talk the talk and walk the walk!)

A few years ago in November, while out on a fun family adventure I unintentionally rode the rapids of the Tallapoosa River in a canoe. This was not the smartest thing I have done in my life, and it did not take long before I ended up in the cold waters of a fast-moving river with my husband, son, and the canoe moving separately and quickly downstream. I had dressed for the cold air above, but the clothes that were keeping me warm above the river filled with water and pulled me under the rapids. I was wearing a life jacket, but that was no match for the weight of the ice-cold water filling my clothes.

Fortunately I am a fairly strong swimmer and was not really far from shore. I swam against the rapids and the undertow and once on shore, I removed the life jacket and then the water-filled coat, only to realize I was on an embankment that had a rock wall rising twenty feet straight up. As I looked down the river to where my family had reached safety, I realized I had to get back in the river and allow the rapids to carry me downstream. I was tired, cold, and at that moment very much afraid. My faith in God and the love for my family overcame the fear and I jumped back in the cold water and was carried to a place of safety by the same rapids that nearly killed me.

Reflecting back on that experience I learned this life lesson: God is in control of the river and it is up to us how we ride it. God has designed a path and a plan for each of us, just like a river. He does not "tell us" what lies ahead, where it will be calm or where we will face the rapids. He provides us with the tools and puts us in the river. Moses so long ago was placed in a basket and put in a river. By God's design the river carried him where he needed to be. How he survived that basket ride we will never know. Maybe he was calm at the rocking of the waves, or maybe he was crying in fear. The river he was in was dangerous in some areas and calm enough to bath in, in others. He did not have to paddle or direct the basket; he simply rode in a basket, with his sister watching along the shore to the place he needed to be.

When riding the river of God's design, how will you

ride it? Anticipating the adventure up ahead? Or kicking and screaming in fear? Will you strive for the balance of God's Word and trust him to carry you through the rapids, or will you stop on the side and dry out before you reach your destiny? God carries us down the river of life regardless of our attitude in the basket or if we overturn it and are moving along in the water (which I might add is not the best way to ride a cold river!).

I am not saying there is a "right way" to ride the river. But God has given us the gift of choice and the fruit of the Spirit to handle whatever the river has to offer. We might make a poor choice along the way, but our choice never changes his love for us or his desire for us to keep moving forward. The path of the river does not depend on my performance on the ride, nor is God's love for us contingent on our performance. He already knows when we will be successful and when we will fail. He knows our pain and when we are cold and afraid. Yet he gently calls us to trust him and stay on the river, knowing that *he* will carry us to a destination of safety.

Chapter 13:

It's Just a Choice, That's All!

Trusting in God's design for our lives requires that we "choose" to be ourselves and allow *him* to be God in us. Having been raised "in the church" as a child, I felt that every decision I made had an eternal consequence. Now it is true that all choices have consequences and that the most important choice we can make is to surrender our lives in obedience to God's word. However, the thought process that every choice I ever make has an influence on eternity becomes a burden that is just too much to bear. For example, if every choice I make "limits God's ability," then who is really "in charge"? Do I really control God?

One Sunday morning, after a challenging message our minister handed out black-and-white bracelets that he encouraged us to wear for at least the week. The black side was to remind us that we can make "wrong choices" and the white side "right choices." During that week, as I focused on the awareness of my choices, I realized that many things I did were simply "just a choice" if I would just lay down all the unnecessary emotional, psychological, and spiritual baggage running through my head.

We do have some "freedom" to choose. "Once these signs are fulfilled, do whatever your hand finds to do, for God is with you"—1 Samuel 10:7. If, however, I let feelings lead the decision, or struggle with every possible intellectual or spiritual ramification of that choice, I will become so burdened by "imaginary responsibility" that the choice grows into a life-changing decision that becomes very hard to make. The agony of the decision process consumes days if not weeks, robs us of sleep, and we get stuck in the mire of indecision.

Philippians 1:21-22 states, "For to me, to live is Christ and to die is gain. If I am to go on living in the body, this will mean fruitful labor for me. Yet what shall I choose? I do not know!" This indicates that living in this body can create positive life experiences. If we are "in Christ" and the desires of our hearts are governed by the Spirit of God, then it is "his" responsibility to manage the outcome of our choices. We are reminded of this in Proverbs 3:5-6: Trust in the LORD with all your heart and lean not on your own understanding; in all your ways acknowledge him, and he will make your paths straight.

And in Proverbs 4:10-12: Listen, my son, accept what I say, and the years of your life will be many. I instruct you in the way of wisdom and lead you along straight paths. When you walk, your steps will not be hampered; when you run, you will not stumble.

Too often we create our own stumbling blocks through indecision, ghosts from the past, imaginary rules, and the need to "feel spiritual" and in "control." Trusting that God is directing the steps that you are taking means letting go of "knowing" all the outcomes before taking every step. Conventional wisdom tells us to "look before you leap," and I agree completely with evaluating our choices and the possible consequences that could follow before making a decision. However, when you have done that, and you have settled into a routine of living as a believer, you should be able to "trust" your choices and the God who is in control of your pathway.

We find in Psalm 20:4: May he give you the desire of your heart and make all your plans succeed.

I have heard many believers interpret these Scriptures as if it means "prosperity" or "external gifts." I think as we attempt to live according to our understanding of the Scriptures, he creates the "desires within the heart" that provide internal direction for our choices. As we trust our choices and his ability to control the pathway we can begin to lay aside some "Christian anxiety" and move toward living in a place of contentment.

But godliness with contentment is great gain. For we brought nothing into the world, and we can take nothing out of it.—I Timothy 6:6-7. Since we can take nothing with us when we leave, the best thing we can do is live a life of contentment that creates a "positive life touch," or what I call "footprints on the heart" of those with whom we have shared this life journey.

Chapter 14:

Fodder for the Vitae

By now you may be thinking I have "thrown out" performance in the life of a believer altogether. I haven't. Clearly there is a place for performance in the life of every believer. Ephesians 4:1 states, I therefore, the prisoner of the Lord, beseech you that ye walk worthy of the vocation wherewith ye are called.

Throughout the Bible, individuals were prepared for a variety of jobs and skills, and all were used by God. It wasn't necessarily the level of education as much as it was that a skill or ability was acquired and that the individual did the job well. As believers, we are all sheep and have but one Shepherd. Where you are located in the flock does not make you "more of a sheep" than anyone else. Some sheep stay in the pen, others are out in the pasture. The position or location of each sheep does not make that sheep more valuable to the Shepherd. When we lose track of our identity as a sheep and begin to build out identity on performance, our "position" becomes our identity. Identity based on performance leads to self-importance with respect to what we are supposed to be doing for God. Have you moved from being a sheep to a "performance identity" of working in the church?

I have often encountered other believers who tell me they are "in the ministry." I generally reply with a smile and a comment that "I live the ministry" (to which they looked confused or quickly walk away). Does God intend for our identity to be based on what we do? Has performance in the church become more valuable than performance at your job? If so, why? I have been blessed to be able to stand on church platforms and sing or teach, and that is a wonderful experience, but it does not compare to holding the hands of a teenager whose arms are red and scarred from cutting while looking her in the eye and telling her she is valuable just because of *who* she is. Or watching countless teenage eyes as they sit in my office, swelling with tears because they felt measured by performance (or lack thereof) and felt worthless. Somehow we have lost the value of a simple life touch to those who are hopeless, and replaced it with "achievement" in the church. The Good Samaritan took his place in the "Will of God" by a simple life touch of meeting the basic needs of the hurting. Can you move through life being a "nameless" caring person who brings an eternal touch to the life of someone who is hurting?

As a university professor, several expectations are part of my position. I have personal continuing education requirements, licensure requirements, university and community service requirements, and performance expectations. I am not exempt from any of those simply because I am "a believer," nor can I perform at a level below my colleagues. My testimony in that world is based on performance. So "work performance" is what I call "fodder for the vitae."

As believers, our "employer" is always God the Father first. If I am there to serve him, my job performance will reflect that. Often many believers forget that their "testimony" is not just the words that come from their mouths but the actions of their hands. Would the hands of Jesus make a "cheap" piece of furniture? I think not. When I work, I do my best unto the Lord. I am not bound by standards of performance that are imaginary or "carved in stone" by someone else. I am there (wherever that may be) to be transparent and allow God's spirit to just flow through me in an activity called "work." That venue has allowed me to teach, travel, serve military families, counsel the hurting, and publish and present research. Some people may say I have accomplished much, but I have simply been Bec. I am trying to live in each moment that God has given me, leaving caring footprints on the lives that cross my path. Maybe they will know my name, maybe not.

The best compliments I have ever received was first from my son, who said, "Mom, if you would do that for strangers, I know you will always be there for me," and later from a young woman who briefly passed through my life. She said, "You are kind of like a spirit, just moving along, touching lives."

Little did she know I am not the Spirit, nor does my touch change lives. I simply allow the Holy Spirit to use this vessel, in each moment of time, riding the river of his design, and when he touches a life, his touch will last an eternity.

Chapter 15:

Footprints on My Heart

O n my life's journey there have been several people who have left footprints on my heart. I think it is important that we remember those who have touched our lives in positive and negative ways, as both are important to personal growth. Scriptures tell us, As iron sharpens iron, so one person sharpens another—Proverbs 27:17.

There have been those who crossed my life path who have brought hurt and betrayal, and yet without that experience, I would not have learned how to move beyond that pain. Carl Jung advocates that what we "see" in others (either negative or positive) is contained to some degree within us. So throughout life, we have opportunities to look in a mirror and check out our own personal growth (or lack thereof) by those who travel though our lives. While I will not name each and every one who has taught me life lessons or supported me while I learned them, I do want to take the time to acknowledge them and the creative work they have facilitated within me.

First, my husband and children who have tolerated my own sometimes egocentric and childish behavior while I was "learning" how to live! They have journeyed with me through all of the joy and pain. They have brought immeasurable joy and laughter and occasionally painful growth experiences. To Kris, who took the picture, and Gunnar, Porter, and Torne' Jacobson who graciously allowed me to use their picture for the cover of this book, thank you. To have each of you as part of my life journey has been a wonderful gift.

To the first young man I counseled so many years ago: you had lost your family and beloved sister in a horrible train accident at fifteen and had to find the courage to face the rest of your life. You wrote poems that turned despair into hope and allowed me to share your pain. That poem remains with me today and reminds me of the importance of touching the lives of others.

To the many teens (who will remained unnamed) who have come through my office over the years since then and honestly shared their pain and loss, I am honored that you trusted me, and you have changed me forever.

Both my breakfast buddy and travel buddy, who have each listened and laughed along with me and have "kvetched" as we lived through life's "trash," your honest feedback provided a mirror to make some much-needed adjustments to my thinking.

My mother who taught me about Jesus probably from the day I was born. My dad, who taught me that you are never too old to repent. My siblings have all taught me lessons, some very hard, which in turn gave me strength that can be poured into the lives of others. You have each played an invaluable part in my life story. My older brother who was willing to give the rough draft of this book a critical read and still had words of encouragement!

To my lifelong friends (I have been blessed to have a few, and you know who you are!), who knew me when I was young and have continued to journey with me in life, and are willing to occasionally revisit the past with me and still accept and love me as Bec. To my ghost who fades in and out of my life reminding me of who I really am, your touch carried me through some rough years.

Thank you to a counselor and colleague, who despite his own life challenges walked beside me through my life experience with betrayal and deceit. Thank you for allowing our Creator to direct your words that still ring true and offer direction.

To the many college professors along my educational journey who challenged my thinking and believed in what I could accomplish (even when I did not).

And finally, thanks to the many prayer warriors and pastors who are faithful to stand in the pulpit, doing their best to care for the body of Christ while at the same time manage their own walk to eternity.

I have been blessed to have so many caring footprints that linger to this day, making me more like the "Bec" God designed me to be. And last but never the least, my caring Savior, who gently guides my basket as I ride the river of life God has designed for me. You have remained faithful even when I am not and have proved your love so many times, in so many different ways. Only you can make beauty from ashes.

And finally, to those of you who read this and in some way are touched, my heart is not that you remember me but that you remember the Creator, who left eternity and walked as a man so that we could follow him home.

References

Arkoff, Abe. *The Illuminated Life*. Needham Heights, MA: Allyn & Bacon, 1995.

Fogarty, J. A. *The Magical Thoughts of Grieving Children*. Amityville, NY: Baywood Publishing Co., 2000.

Gospel Communications, BibleGateway,com, March 2007, http://www.biblegateway.com/

Hart, A. D. *The Anxiety Cure*. Thomas Nelson Publishers, USA, 1999.

Landreth, G. L. *Play Therapy: The Art of the Relationship*. New York, NY: Brunner-Routledge, 2002.

Leman. K.. *The Birth Order Book*. New York, NY: Dell Publishing, 1985.

Leonard, B. E. "Stress, Norepinephrine, and Depression." *Journal of Psychiatry & Neuroscience*. Ottawa. Vol. 26, pp. S11-17. \

http://proquest.umi.com.libproxy.troy.edu/pqdweb?index=10 &did=83205532&SrchMode=1&sid=12&Fmt=4&VInst =PROD&VType=PQD&RQT=309&VName=PQD&T S=1205425738&clientId=15382

Lewis, C. S. *The Inspirational Writings of C. S. Lewis*. New York, NY: Inspirational Press (1994).

Nichols M. P. and Schwartz R. C. *Family Therapy: Concepts and Methods*. Needham Heights, MA: Allyn & Bacon, 1998.

Seniors Devotional Bible, New International Version. Grand Rapids Michigan: Zondervan Publishing House, 1996.

Smalley G. and Trent J. *The Blessing*. New York, NY: Simon & Schuster, 1990.

Smith S. and Pergola J. "Stress Management: Strategies for Individuals." University of Florida, IFAS Extension. http://edis.ifas.ufl.edu, 2006.

Wade, N. "Introduction to the Special Issue on Forgiveness in Therapy." *Journal of Mental Health Counseling*, 32(1), 1-4. Retrieved April 19, 2011, from Research Library.

Appendix

1. This document is FCS2077A, one of a series of the Family, Youth and Community Sciences Department, Florida Cooperative Extension Service, Institute of Food and Agricultural Sciences, University of Florida. Original publication date February 27, 2003. Revised May 11, 2006. Visit the EDIS Web Site at http://edis.ifas.ufl.edu.

2. Suzanna Smith, associate professor, Human Development, Department of Family, Youth and Community Sciences, and Joe Pergola, extension agent IV, Hillsborough County, Florida Cooperative Extension Service, IFAS, University of Florida, Gainesville FL 32611.

About the Author

D r. Rebecca Jacobson is the youngest of eight children, born in Baltimore, Md and raised in Florida. She is married and has 3 sons, two of which are married. She taught counseling and psychology courses for 12 years at Troy University, before retiring to run her private practice and consulting business. She has several research publications and has served on the Board of the Alabama Association for Play Therapy, as faculty for Capella University and as a Military Family Life Consultant. She has a Masters degree in psychology and received her Ph.D. in educational psychology in 2000 from Auburn University. She continued her education to become a licensed counselor, a nationally certified counselor and a registered play therapist. She continues to provide workshops and research presentations at both National and International conferences and serves as a Program Coordinator for the Alabama National Guard.

CPSIA information can be obtained at www.ICGtesting.com
Printed in the USA
LVOW062016300911

248617LV00002B/1/P

9 781462 706143